Death And Illness

THE FAMILY

DEATH AND ILLNESS

by
Leslie McGuire

The Rourke Corporation, Inc.

The Rourke Corporation, Inc.
P.O. Box 3328, Vero Beach, FL 32964

McGuire, Leslie, 1945-
     Death And illness / by Leslie McGuire.
        p.   cm. — (The Family)
     Includes index.
     Summary: Describes what it is like to have a loved one face a terminal illness or die suddenly, depicting the experiences of various young people in this situation and how they felt.
     ISBN 0-86593-079-1
     1. Death—Juvenile literature. 2. Bereavement—Juvenile literature. 3. Terminally ill— Juvenile literature. [1. Death. 2. Terminally ill.] I. Title. II. Series: Family (Vero Beach, Fla.)
     HQ1073.3.M39   1990
     155.9'37—dc 20   90-8740
                                                                                          CIP
                                                                                          AC

Series Editor: Gregory Lee
Editors: Elizabeth Sirimarco, Marguerite Aronowitz
Book design and production: The Creative Spark,
     Capistrano Beach, CA
Cover illustration: Rob Court

Death And Illness

Contents

I. Death And Young People

Anyone who begins reading a book about death and illness might expect it to be very depressing. But there is one thing you learn when talking to people who are very sick or dying. You learn that life is wonderful, and that every moment should be appreciated—even if some of those moments are less than wonderful. It's true: People who are very sick are often able to enjoy many of their days. People who have accepted the fact that they are dying are not always depressed.

This book is for the survivors. The very word survivor has many meanings. It could mean that you are the one still alive after someone you love has died. It could also mean that you have the capacity to survive even the most upsetting experiences and get on with your life.

It is in the last sense that this book is written—to help young people cope with the death of someone close to them, or even perhaps their own death. This book is also written to help people face

•
A memorial service sometimes includes a viewing of the body by any who wish to pay their respects to the deceased. The body "lies in state" in a coffin as friends and relatives file past.
•

and deal with the severe illness of someone they love and respect or help people deal with an illness of their own.

That is not to say that a person can keep from experiencing grief or sadness. Grieving is the normal way people deal with loss, and the fact that one is grieving is not by itself depressing. It is not dealing with the loss of a loved one that causes the most damage.

Young people often have an especially difficult time dealing with the death of someone close to them, but most adults also have a hard time. Historically, we see that people have always been afraid of death. Psychiatrists say this is because our minds cannot understand or comprehend the possibility of our own death, and we cannot be certain what happens after we die. Since everything we see, do, and experience is part of ourselves, it is difficult to think that these things will continue on without us.

Trying To Understand Death

The easiest way our minds can begin to think about death is if we see it as coming from some terrible accident. For example, if a car goes off a cliff, that ends everything. But the concept of a slow, deadly disease, or even old age is far more difficult to grasp. An accident is terrible, but there is a cause even though it may be a random one. A terminal illness is harder to deal with because its cause is invisible.

Because we often see death as a catastrophe, we tend to look at it as frightening. Death is associated with a very bad experience. It is not considered to be a process or a part of life.

If adults cannot understand or cope with death, how can they explain it to children? Small children do not come into the world with a fear of death. They are born with only two innate fears: fear of falling from high places, and fear of loud noises. Other fears we have as we grow up are learned from people around us.

Another thing about death that is hard to

comprehend is its finality. When you are young, you have a sense of immortality. Sure, some day you will get old and die. But that is so very far away, it is practically meaningless. You watch television, and people die all the time. It is usually something that happens to other people—not to you or someone you know.

Throughout history, in cultures around the world, people have defined ways to cope with death. Every culture has tried to discover ways for its people to accept death and go on living. The ancient Egyptians buried their loved ones with all the things they needed and loved in life so that they would have everything with them in the afterlife. The Egyptians believed that death was merely another place, another part of a dead person's spiritual path.

The concept of an afterlife is part of most religions. Religions can believe in heaven and hell, reincarnation, or a special spirit world that mirrors the world of the living. This is one popular tool that people use to try to cope with death.

The role that religion plays in today's family, however, is different from what it used to be. As science and technology become more advanced, religion seems to be losing some of its power over people's everyday lives. This may be one of the things that makes it especially hard for people to cope with death in today's world. Science and technology have almost become a new religion in themselves because they focus on keeping people alive. It is easy to ignore the fact that everyone will eventually have to die when new medicines are always being discovered, new machines are invented, and new life prolonging procedures continue to be tried. Is it any wonder then, that death creates so many problems for the survivors?

Death And Guilt

There is often a lot of guilt surrounding someone's death. For example, a husband and

Death is difficult for anyone to accept, but children especially need to understand the reality of death and be allowed to share in the grieving process.

•

wife may have fought all the time they were married. If the wife dies, the husband feels terrible because he never said all the kind things he was thinking or did anything special for her. Or a child may get angry at a parent or grandparent and think, "I wish he were dead!" If that person dies, there is often the guilty feeling that the wish became reality. But wishes are not facts, and feelings do not create reality like magic.

There can also be a lot of anger at a person

who dies. A child whose mother dies may be furious with her for leaving. He or she feels abandoned. "How could she do this to me when I still need her?" Then the child feels guilty for being so angry at someone they loved so much.

A lot of these conflicting feelings come from the way we talk about death. People find it very hard to put their feelings into words, and most people are afraid to even think about their own deaths. They say things like, "Why talk about something so depressing?" when what they really mean is, "Why talk about something so frightening?"

Talking About Death

There are many ways to avoid talking about death. One of the silliest is the choice of words people use when they have to discuss it. Instead of just saying that someone died, you'll hear people say things like, "he passed on" or "she left us," or "they are with the angels now." Sometimes parents will say, "Grandma's sleeping," or "she went to be with Grandpa." People seem to think that using a *euphemism* (a substitute word) for death will make it easier to handle. The fact is that these words only make death harder to understand, especially for children.

For example, if a small child is told that Grandma is just sleeping, he or she may be terrified of going to sleep. If a young boy is told that his father is now with Grandpa, he will feel abandoned by his father. Why would Daddy want to be with Grandpa more than him?

Once a young person understands the finality of death, they may become afraid that other people they love will also die. If a child's father dies, they may start worrying that their mother will die, too. This often happens when a grandparent dies. The child sees how sad his parent feels and becomes concerned about how it would be if their mom or dad were to die.

But all these feelings are perfectly natural. Human beings have been feeling them since time began.

Fear, guilt, anger and abandonment have always been part of human nature. They may be part of the reason adults try to hide the facts about death from their children. But death is not an easy thing to hide. If a mother "goes to heaven" and never comes back, the child can't help but wonder why he or she has been left alone. The complete loss can really be explained in only one way—with the truth.

Marybeth

Marybeth was only 17 years old when she was diagnosed as having leukemia. Leukemia is a form of cancer that usually shortens a person's life drastically. But Marybeth had every intention of living for a long, long time, despite what her doctors told her. "There is probably no way I can live much past the age of one hundred and sixty," she said with a laugh. But no matter how hard she tried, and how much more the doctors learned about ways to treat leukemia, she still had to face the fact that there was a limit to her life span. Of course, that did not mean that she could not live to be a ripe old age, but she said that having this illness did give her a lot of perspective. She kept saying, "Well, I'm seventeen, and that means I only have a hundred and forty-three years left. It's not very long, but I intend to make the most of it."

Marybeth was not denying death or giving up hope. She had every intention of living her life to the fullest, regardless of how long it lasted. She also had a lot to teach most people about life, because she understood death.

Coping With Death

One of the best ways to cope with the death of someone you love is to let yourself feel all the grief and sadness you can. Funerals, periods of mourning, wearing black or an armband, relying on friends and family for help, talking about how you feel, and crying when you feel like it are all ways of releasing the grief and confusing emotions felt after the loss of someone close to you.

Every human being has a right to their feelings and their sense of dignity. By not allowing ourselves to feel sadness, we are denying ourselves the right to feel love. And loving is the most human thing that people do between birth and death. We also have as much right to die with dignity as we do to live with dignity. If death is not accepted, then someone who is dying is not accepted either. Perhaps the saddest part of today's wish to deny death is the way we deal with people who are very sick or who are dying.

Very often the terminally ill become a source of either embarrassment or fear to their families and friends. We stay away from them. We try to keep our children away from them. And instead of showing personal concern, we stand back while health care professionals help them cope with the ends of their lives. Yet every time we deny someone the right to his or her dignity and humanity, we also deny our own dignity and humanity. It is possible that someday we too will be in a sterile hospital room surrounded by professional people who are caring, but do not love us. And that is a terrible trend to set in motion. For no matter who we are or what our age, it is a sad thing to leave this world without someone we love by our side.

II. The Death Of Someone You Love

Jillian was in eighth grade. She had a very busy schedule. She played soccer, took piano and ballet lessons, and spent time with friends after school. She had homework in the evenings. One day when she got home, there was a note from her mother saying, "Casserole in the fridge, be home around ten." Jillian's parents sometimes went out in the evening, and Jillian could easily take care of herself. Besides, it was fun to be able to talk on the phone for hours without hearing any remarks about getting her homework done.

The next morning Jillian's mother woke her and said, "Grandma died last night. The funeral is tomorrow, but you don't have to come." Jillian was shocked. She had never thought her grandma

A hospice is a special facility for terminally ill patients where family members can room with the person who is dying. The emphasis is on homelike care, instead of the life-prolonging mechanisms of a hospital.

would die.

When she was a small child, her grandmother had lived with them. Her mother and father both worked, so it was grandmother who took care of her, read her stories, taught her how to make chocolate chip cookies, and took her to the park to play.

Eventually Jillian's grandmother had moved to a small apartment of her own, and just recently she decided to move into a retirement home not too far away. Jillian visited her now and then, always remembering to bring some of her own chocolate chip cookies.

Later Jillian talked about how she'd been told of her grandmother's death. "It was the same as if she'd been shot in the street," she said. "I didn't even know she was sick."

Jillian's mother hadn't meant to shut her out. But when Jillian asked why she hadn't been told her grandma was sick, her mother replied, "We didn't want to upset you."

When Jillian's mother told her that she didn't have to come to the funeral, Jillian felt even more shut out of the process. She insisted on going to the funeral, but afterward, when relatives came over to their house, the adults seemed to ignore her. Her father finally said, "Why don't you go watch television?"

"We thought it would upset her to see people crying, especially her mother," said Jillian's father.

In fact, Jillian felt like she was being told her love for her grandmother wasn't important. No one understood that she needed to cry also. They were acting like Jillian's love and grief were less important than their emotions. Jillian had wanted to say goodbye to her grandmother, and she was furious that no one took her to visit her before she died.

When she tried to talk to her best friend about what happened, her friend said, "Gee, that's too bad," and then started talking about something else. It took Jillian almost a year to stop feeling angry at her mother and father and stop wanting to turn back the clock.

Jillian finally convinced her parents to take her to the cemetary where she placed a bunch of daisies and a paper plate with four chocolate chip cookies below the headstone. Jillian felt much better, but she said, "It would have been so much easier if they had let me do everything I'd wanted at the right time."

Joey

Joey was visiting his relatives for the summer. The whole family lived on a large farm in a remote part of South Dakota. It was a place that Joey really loved, and he had visited there every year since he could remember. That summer, Joey's great uncle Bill—whose farm it had been before his children started running it—had a bad fall. Uncle Bill was a very active 80-year-old who had always liked Joey.

The injured man was carried into the house, and a doctor was called to come to the house. The nearest hospital was about 70 miles away. The doctor did not have very good news. He said that Uncle Bill probably wouldn't make it, but that he thought it would be a good idea to have an ambulance take him to the hospital where he could receive better care until he died.

Uncle Bill, however, said he would rather die at home. His wish was granted. Even though he was very weak and in a lot of pain, Bill asked that all the other members of his family be invited to come to his bedside. People were called on the telephone and started arriving within hours. Everyone went in to talk with him, including Joey.

That night, Uncle Bill died in his own bed. He had wanted his funeral held in the house, and he wanted to be buried in the apple grove behind the house. All of these things were done. Even though everyone was very sad, and even though everyone knew they would miss him terribly, no one tried to cover up how they felt or deny what was happening.

Joey was shocked at first. "It was hard to

talk to him, because you could see how much he was hurting," Joey said. "But he told me how much he liked me, and hoped I would grow up and stay as smart as I already was even though I lived in the city most of the year."

Joey was included in all phases of the old man's death and funeral. He saw the body laid out in the living room. He watched everyone cry, and Joey did, too.

"But, you know, I could see that he was really dead, once he was gone. His color was different. Sort of greyish. I also saw how much pain he was in. I knew that no matter what they did to him in the hospital, he wouldn't have felt much better unless he was drugged to sleep or something."

The old man had a chance to say goodbye to all his family. In return, everyone in the family, right down to the smallest child, was able to understand his death. There would be no fears that he had abandoned them on purpose, and no guilt that they had left things unsaid.

"I think I realized for the first time that people die and that it's okay," said Joey. "I mean, he knew he was dying, and he didn't go nuts or anything. He just said everything he had to say, and then allowed himself to leave us in a really nice way."

A Couple Of Facts About Death

Most Common

The most common cause of death in the United States is major cardiovascular (heart) disease, which claims its victims at a rate of 395.5 deaths per 100,000 of the population. Second is all combined forms of cancer, with a mortality rate of 198.6 deaths per 100,000 people. Tied for third are pneumonia and all forms of accidental death, including automobile accidents (between 20 and 30 deaths per 100,000).

By State

By far the highest death rate in the United States today is in Washington, D.C., with a rate in 1987 of 13.8 deaths per 1,000 persons, followed closely by Florida, Missouri, Pennsylvania, Rhode Island, Tennessee and West Virginia with averages of 10 deaths per 1,000 per year. The states with the lowest annual death rate are Hawaii, Colorado, Utah, Wyoming and—the winner—Alaska, at 4.0 deaths per 1,000.

The highest motor vehicle death rates are in Arizona, Mississippi, New Mexico and South Carolina. North Dakota, Massachusetts, and Washington, D.C., have the lowest automobile death rates.

Source: Department of Health and Human Services National Center for Health Statistics

Sarah was only 11 years old when her father became very sick with cancer. Sarah's mother wanted to spend every evening at the hospital with him, but she didn't know what to do with Sarah. She was too young to stay home by herself, and there weren't any neighbors or friends close enough for her to stay with.

Even though Sarah's mother was upset by the idea, she had no choice but to let Sarah come to the hospital every day after school.

Fortunately for Sarah and her parents, some of the doctors at the hospital were very sympathetic. Sarah's father had been given about six weeks to live. He was in the terminal ward, and under ordinary circumstances children weren't allowed to go into those rooms. But since the hospital wasn't too crowded, he had a room to himself.

Sarah was allowed to sit with him for several hours every day. She brought her homework with her, and he would help her with parts of her work.

As he got closer and closer to death, Sarah's father was less inclined to talk. He was also in a great deal of pain and had to be sedated with a drug called morphine. Sometimes the morphine gave him daydreams that were a lot like nightmares. He would cry out, frightened.

"It was like he was a little kid," Sarah said. "One day he tried to sit up. He kept saying, 'Why did you put plywood over the windows? Why won't you let me see out? Take it down, it's so dark in here!' It made me very sad."

Sarah was frightened, but she was not afraid to talk to the doctors. She asked one of the doctors why her father was so afraid. The doctor explained that sometimes morphine did that to people. Sarah thought for a moment, then asked, "Could you give him another kind so he won't be so scared?" The doctor was surprised, but he said they would try something else and see if it would help stop the nightmares. In fact, it did.

On the day that Sarah's father died, Sarah and her mother had gone out to get some dinner. They were both so tired and unhappy that they decided to go to a nice restaurant instead of the hospital cafeteria. When they returned, one of the residents stopped them in the hall. "I'm sorry," he said, "but he's passed away."

Sarah's first thought was that he had been taken already out of the room. She started to cry, because she hadn't really said goodbye. She also felt guilty because she and her mother had been eating a nice dinner while he was dying. She wished she could take back the dinner, and she never wanted to see that restaurant again.

"But you know," she said a few weeks later, "I realized that maybe he was waiting for us to leave so he could die. And I also realized that all those nights in the hospital we had been saying goodbye to each other. He was still my Dad, and it was good that I was there while he was still conscious. He knew that I loved him, and I guess maybe he felt really bad about dying on me. Maybe he wanted to, but he just couldn't while I was there."

Sarah and Joey were allowed to share the many aspects of death. In Joey's case, this was deliberate. In Sarah's, her mother didn't know what else to do. Both of those children were involved in the funeral as well.

Sarah's mother had so many things to do immediately after her father died that she didn't have much time for Sarah. But what she did do was give Sarah tasks of her own. Since they wanted music at the funeral, she asked Sarah to make a tape of whatever music she felt was right for the service. Sarah spent hours going through her father's records. Eventually she picked out some music by Bach that was both simple and joyous. She knew it had been one of her father's favorites.

Sarah also got to choose the flowers. One night she sat down and wrote her father a letter telling him how much he had meant to her. Her mother was very moved by it, and asked the pastor to read it at the funeral service.

Sarah missed her father terribly. But she was able to work through some of her grief in a way that made her much more mature and helped lessen her pain.

Jillian, on the other hand, was not really allowed to participate in any of the circumstances surrounding her grandmother's death. It took her a long time to work through much of the guilt and anger she felt, and both of these emotions made her sadness much harder to deal with.

Joey was lucky enough to see what it was like for someone old to die at home, surrounded by his family. It helped Joey understand that death is a natural part of life. It also made it less threatening to him, and now Joey has less fear of death. He accepts it. He also likes to think about his great uncle Bill's wish that he grow up "normal" despite modern-day pressures on him.

"I guess he was trying to tell me that living in the city means you get separated from everything in nature," Joey said. "It doesn't have to mean that unless you let it happen. That's kind of what happened to him when he died at home. It was more natural than going to some hospital."

III. What We Can Learn From The Dying

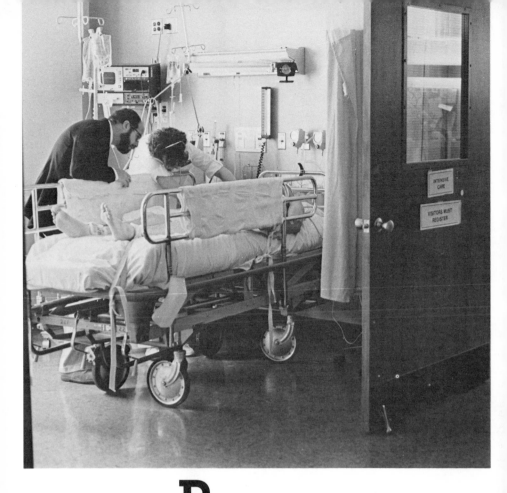

People of all ages who are dying have many things to teach us. A lesson in dying gracefully can be a lesson in living gracefully.

It isn't only the people who are trying to cope with the death of a loved one who need help. People who are dying also need to talk about what is happening to them. They need to share their fears and thoughts but they usually worry that discussing it will upset the people who love them. Often the dying feel that they are no longer being treated like real people.

When someone you love is seriously ill, they may have to stay in a hospital for days or weeks. Visiting hospital wards is difficult for some people because they don't like to see reminders of illness and death.

Jenna

Jenna's grandfather was at home when he felt a terrible tightening in his chest. Jenna's mother called 911, and grandfather was rushed to the hospital in an ambulance. From the moment the paramedics came, what happened to Jenna's grandfather was no longer under his control or that of the family. All Jenna and her mother could do was hold each other's hands and watch as grandfather was placed on the stretcher and wheeled quickly out of the house into the hands of medical people in an ambulance with a screaming siren.

When he reached the hospital there were noises, bright lights, pumps, and loud voices all around. He was surrounded by nurses, orderlies, doctors, interns, and lab technicians. He was rushed to X-ray. He was plugged into monitors. He had tubes put in his nose and mouth. He was taken into intensive care.

From the moment he left the house, Jenna's grandfather was no longer treated like a person. It was as if he had no choice as to what would be done to him. He knew everyone was trying to save his life; they were around him all the time, working constantly. They were busy with his heart rate, his pulse, his electrocardiogram, his secretions, and his pulmonary functions. No one had time for his feelings. No one had time to answer any of his questions.

In recent years, society—through medical technology and doctors—has been dealing with death by trying to prevent it or extending it as long as possible through any means possible. At a certain point in everyone's life, however, death is inevitable. People of all ages need help accepting that.

Brenda found out she had cancer during the last few weeks of her senior year in high school. One morning she had a swollen gland in her neck, and the next thing she knew she was diagnosed as having leukemia.

"I couldn't believe it," she said. "I was going to college, I was in the tennis tournament, I had a great date for the prom—I didn't have time for this!"

Her family was stunned, and her three

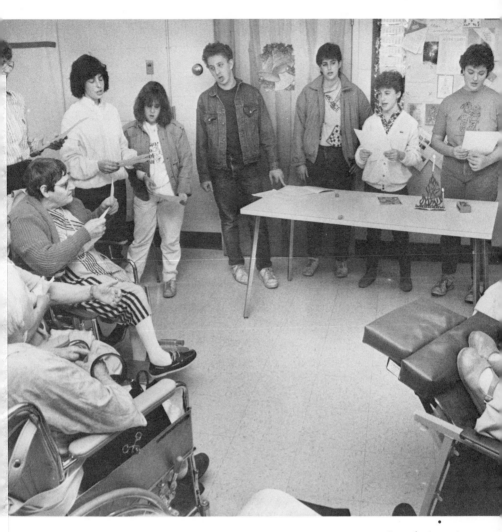

younger brothers and sisters were frightened.

"When the doctor told us what I had and what my chances were, I asked my parents to leave me alone with him," said Brenda. "I had a lot of questions I had to ask. I knew my parents wouldn't be able to handle either the questions or the answers. But I also knew I had to have as much information as I could get without all the emotional stuff. I mean, this was real! I had a battle on my hands that was totally serious, and I couldn't let their fear and worry for me get in the way."

Brenda had the right attitude. She knew that her family would try to protect her. After all, she

In today's society we often isolate those who have grown too old to care for themselves, or who are dying. "Nursing homes" or "rest homes" are places where many elderly live their final years alone. These youths are combatting this isolation by visiting such a home to sing songs.

was still their child, and they didn't want anything to hurt her. But she felt she had to know everything she could, otherwise she wouldn't be able to fight it. She also needed to know what her chances were of surviving. There was a real possibility that she would lose the fight, and she had to deal realistically with that, too.

"Oh, yeah, there were some rough moments," she said. "The chemotherapy makes you so sick, and when my hair finally fell out I almost wished I were dead. But then I realized what that meant. I remembered all the times I'd gotten mad or upset and said, 'I wish I were dead!' I realized that wasn't true at all. I really wanted to be alive—more than anything in the world."

Brenda's leukemia went into remission, but came back again 18 months later. She had to start chemotherapy all over again. But Brenda had made up her mind to fight, and she did.

A young boy she knew from the hospital named George decided not to fight anymore when his cancer came back for the third time. His parents were angry and hurt, but George said no. He didn't want to go through the agony again. He elected to die calmly and gracefully, in full control, after having said goodby to his family and friends. It may sound kind of magical, and in a way it was magical. This choice is one that all people should be allowed to make.

Johnny

Johnny's father had brain cancer. All the neighbors and his teachers knew. His friend's parents said that Johnny was going through a hard time. Soon it felt as if people were walking on eggshells around him. Soon, they started avoiding him.

"I guess everyone felt they didn't know what to say to me, so they decided not to say anything at all," said Johnny. "But that kind of made it harder.

"One kid at school even said he didn't want to sit next to me because he thought he

Coping with grief is never easy, and sometimes waiting for a person to die—or get well—causes many different emotions, from sadness to anger.

would catch it. Well, if I hadn't caught it, then how could he?"

But Johnny said that catching it was one of the things he had worried about at first, too.

"The doctor had to explain that brain cancer wasn't something you could catch like a cold," said Johnny. "He and my mother saw that I didn't want to visit Dad. It even took me a while to figure out what was bothering me, so I guess I can understand how other people feel —especially when they don't know the facts."

Brenda and Johnny can help us understand how powerful the fear of death or dying is. This fear often ends up making everything harder for the person who is sick or dying. In Brenda's case, she needed to talk to her doctor alone because she felt her family couldn't accept what was happening to her and would deny her need to ask all the questions she needed to ask. So she had to do something very difficult by herself.

Denying death is something everyone goes through at one time or another. But sometimes denying the possibility of dying makes people even sicker. For example, some wait to get help until it is

Some Thoughts About Death

And our hearts...like muffled drums, are beating funeral marches to the grave.
—Henry Wadsworth Longfellow

Life does not cease to be funny when people die any more than it ceases to be serious when people laugh.
—George Bernard Shaw

There is no constitutional right to choose to die.
—Chief Justice Joseph Weintraub,
New Jersey Supreme Court

But at my back I always hear
Time's winged chariot hurrying near.
—Andrew Marvell

A man's death is more the survivors' affair than his own.
—Thomas Mann

Those who welcome death have only tried it from the ears up.
—Wilson Mizner

Even though I walk through the valley
of the shadow of death,
I fear no evil...
—Psalms 23:4

I'm not afraid to die. I just don't want to be there when it happens.
—Woody Allen

too late for any possible cure to work. How much better it would be if everyone could accept death as a necessary part of life, do what they can to prevent it from coming too soon, and try to prepare themselves and their families for what will be inevitable at some time in their lives.

Johnny was isolated from his friends because of their fear and lack of understanding. George decided to do his best, then accepted his own death with grace. Brenda elected to fight, and eventually she won. In each of these cases, their decisions would have been much easier to make if the fear felt by the people around them had been kept under control.

IV. Facing Death

People facing death go through a number of different emotions once they are told the news. Sociologist Dr. Elisabeth Kubler-Ross identifies the five stages of death: denial, anger, bargaining, depression, and finally acceptance. Family members and friends will also go through these five stages.

Denial

The first stage is when the patient says, "It isn't true. This simply can't be happening to me." Almost everyone reacts that way initially. It is a healthy way of handling very shocking and painful news. It gives human beings time to collect themselves in an orderly way so they can effectively deal with the information later on. When someone is in the denial stage, they don't want to hear any more information or talk about death. But later, they are relieved—even happy—to have a chance to sit and talk to someone about what is happening to them. Family and friends should understand this and wait for the dying person to be ready to talk.

An outsider may be upset at the thought of discussing someone's death with them but this reluctance to talk merely supports the denial stage, and makes it harder for the dying person to cope with their situation. Of course, most people don't want to talk about death. They are experiencing their own kind of denial.

Anger

The second stage is anger—when someone realizes he or she is dying and gets angry. They might say, "Why me? Why couldn't this have happened to somebody else?" This stage is the hardest for the family, because the anger gets directed toward the people close by. For example, the dying person may get angry at the doctors, the hospital staff, and family members. He or she is probably trying to say, "I'm not dead yet!"

Sometimes people are so terrified by having

to be close to someone who is dying, that they almost wish they would just hurry up and die. Then they wouldn't have to think about it any more, and they wouldn't have to pay any more attention to what the process of dying is really like. They want desperately to get away from the dying person. Of course, this makes someone who is dying feel even worse. To prove they are still alive, they will even complain more.

But it is important that people close to a dying person try to tolerate this difficult behavior. There is a great deal of relief in expressing one's anger and frustration.

Bargaining

The third stage is called bargaining. This isn't a stage we usually see because it is very private. Once a person has denied that death is near, accepted that it is true and then gotten angry about it, it is only natural that this person will try to postpone death by making a deal. It's like a small child saying, "If I keep my room really clean for a week and eat all my vegetables, will you let me go to the zoo?"

A recent study has shown that there is a 35 percent decrease in death rates among elderly Chinese women right before important family holidays. Then right after the holidays, there is a 35 percent increase in the death rate before it returns to normal. What does this mean? Many people who are dying want to live long enough to attend a family function, see a child get married, or be alive when a baby is born. Somehow they manage to hang on until the event occurs, then they let go and die.

This is a form of "short-term bargaining." Others may say things such as, "I will devote my life to good works if only you let me live." This is known as bargaining with God.

These promises can also come from feelings of guilt. A person may see his or her death as punishment for some sin, rather than as an incurable disease or the natural aging of the body and

At memorial services or funerals, friends and family gather to remember and say goodbye to a loved one who has died. Grieving is a natural, healthy human emotion, one that helps heal the pain of the loss.

its inevitable death.

Depression

The fourth stage is depression. There are two kinds of depression a very ill person faces. One is caused by sadness and guilt about money, time lost from work, and difficulties that will be faced by the people they are leaving behind such as old people, beloved children, or spouses. This depression can be dealt with by taking care of the problems. For example, a house can be sold to get more money, and child care can be found for children. A household can also be reorganized to make things easier on a husband or wife.

The second kind of depression comes from a person truly having to say goodbye to his or her life. Usually when you are around someone who is sad, you try to cheer them up. But just cheering a person up with happy talk doesn't give them anything to help them deal with the fact that they are losing everything they've come to know and love.

People who are dying have to be allowed to express their sorrow. That is the only way they will be able to accept death more easily. Families can help by listening, and letting the person talk as much as they want. It doesn't help to tell them things that should cheer them up. This kind of depression is necessary to help a dying person come to terms with what is happening. It allows them to die in peace.

Acceptance

The fifth and final stage is acceptance. This isn't a happy stage, but more like a numbness. It means that the painful struggle is over, and that the dying person wants peace and quiet. He or she needs to have their hand held, and they just want to know that someone is with them.

People who are dying usually want to have physical contact with people they love. If someone is in an oxygen tent or full of tubes and wires and obviously in pain, however, this can be difficult. But human beings thrive on hugging, hand holding and physical warmth. When they are dying, this very important form of comforting often gets taken away.

Moira

When Moira was told that her mother was dying, she couldn't believe it. Her mother had checked into the hospital for tests for what her doctors originally thought was a nasty virus. But it turned out that instead she had a very fast-growing form of cancer, and only had about eight weeks to live.

Moira and her mother had always been very close. Both of them tried to be brave. Neither of them cried, and Moira's mother simply said, "Well, I guess that's that." Moira could think of nothing to say. She didn't want to lose her mother any more than her mother wanted to die. But there was clearly nothing more anyone could do.

One day Moira was visiting her mother in the hospital. She was exhausted and unhappy about having to sit in the hard, uncomfortable chair next to her mother's bed. As she looked at the small, isolated figure of her mother lying in the center of the bed, Moira felt like crawling in and lying down.

"I just decided the heck with all the conventions in hospitals," she said. "That bed was big enough for two, and I really needed my mommy to hug me. So I just climbed in with her. We put our arms around each other and held on for dear life. It made her feel better, and it made me feel better, too."

Both the people who are dying and the people who they are leaving behind need more comfort than they ever did before. The way that Moira chose to help herself was a way that helped her mother, too.

"The funniest part," Moira said, "was one day when a whole flying wedge of residents and interns came into the room with their clipboards and their serious faces. They couldn't believe what they were seeing. I finally told them, 'One of us is really sick, and the other one is just fine. If you can figure out which one is which, they'll let you stay on staff. If not, you get fired.' Mother and I started giggling, but not one of them cracked a smile."

Coming To Terms With Death

When someone is facing death, there are many coping methods to help both the dying person and his or her family and friends come to terms with death. Some are effective, and some aren't. Some people are supported by their families, but some families get stuck in the denial phase, which makes it very hard for the dying person.

Religion can play a very significant part in helping people deal with death. Religion often provides comfort for the dying and helps survivors handle their grief.

Different religions have different ways of dealing with death. Some religions believe there is an afterlife—the idea that the spirit or soul lives on in a purer and happier form, or that there is a heaven where peace and love wait for those who die. There is also the belief that people will be reunited with loved ones who have died before them, that they will see their mother or father or grandparents again. Although they are sad to be dying, people who believe this are comforted by the thought that they will be once again with a beloved parent, spouse, sister or brother.

Other people believe there is a spirit world that mirrors the one on earth. Ancient Egyptians believed this, and buried their dead with all the important things they would need in the afterlife. Wealthy people were even buried with things like pleasure boats, fully set tables with lots of food and—unfortunately—their servants and household pets as well.

Belief in reincarnation also comforts many people facing death. They believe that their time on earth is merely one stage in their total existence and that they will keep coming back time and again as either another person or something entire

different. These people believe they will get to ve over and over again, so there is nothing really ɔ grieve about.

he Funeral

Funeral services vary among different fami-es, religions and cultures. Sometimes the body is isplayed in an open coffin at a funeral home or a hurch. Sometimes the coffin is closed. Sometimes ne body is not buried but cremated. The ashes re either placed in a ceremonial urn (vase), or cattered over a place chosen by the person who ied. Sometimes the ashes are scattered over the cean or a place chosen by the person's surviving mily.

A funeral is a sad affair, but it can also be a way to celebrate the life of the deceased. In this traditional New Orleans funeral, fellow jazz musicians march and play for their lost comrade.

Todd

Todd's grandfather loved the ocean, and especially the bay. He took his boat out almost every day to fish, or just sat and watched the waves and the sky. When he died, his family chose to scatter his ashes on the bay. They felt he would be happiest knowing that his ashes were spending eternity in his beloved body of water. Even though they held a formal memorial service to which all grandfather's friends had been invited, they held their own private ceremony with only the family present on the day they scattered the ashes.

Funeral services often include relatives and friends telling the congregation about the person who died. At Todd's grandfather's memorial service, several people spoke about how kind he was and all the good things he did. This is called a eulogy. Todd's grandfather's life had touched a lot of people and affected many people around him. Eulogies help people understand that although death may feel like a waste, the life that preceded it certainly was anything but that.

Grief As Healing

The one thing that helps people go on living after the death of someone they love is grieving. Everyone has a right to grieve, regardless of how old they are. A little child should be included in the process just as much as an older person. Most people know how bad it feels to lose someone they love. Hiding one's feelings does not make them go away. Adults should not try to hide their grief from themselves or those around them. Doing so can make a person sick both physically and psychologically.

Acknowledging grief is the same as acknowledging other emotions like anger or love. If you take away a person's experience of loss, that person will suffer and become poorer in spirit. No one would want another person to be unable to feel love, would they? And yet that is almost what they are asking when they don't approve showing their feelings of fear, loss or pain. They are saying

This doesn't upset me. Why should it upset you?" Or, "I'm going to be brave and not let anyone see I'm sad." Or, "Guys aren't supposed to cry."

Grieving is healthy. It is the human way for the body and mind to take care of sadness and shock.

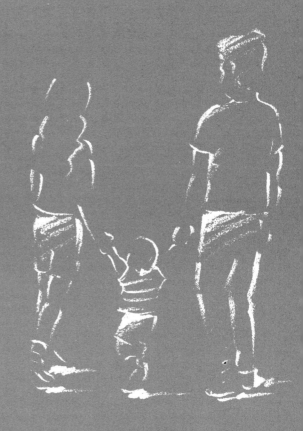

V. Facing
A Serious
Illness

Sometimes a serious illness or freak accident changes a young person's life completely. It isn't that life ends, but it certainly changes the way you understood it before. For example, a chronic illness like cancer or leukemia can take away someone's ability to function on their normal level.

Survival rates for many diseases that used to kill people have gone up considerably since 1962. For Hodgkins disease, the survival rate has climbed from 50 to 90 percent. For bone cancer, it has gone up from 20 to 60 percent; for retinoblastoma, from 78 to 90 percent; for non-Hodgkin's lymphoma, from 6 to 80 percent; and for acute lymphocytic leukemia from 0 to 60 percent. These are exciting and wonderful statistics. But behind these statistics are many young people who have had their lives changed forever by serious illness.

Every day children with life-threatening diseases face things that would make a strong man cry. Yet they keep going, keep trying, keep living, and also keep making jokes.

Some Personal Stories

"Humor is what keeps me going," said Stephen, who has had to go through the full course of chemotherapy three times. "When people ask me what happened to my hair, I tell them I do drugs. I just don't tell them which ones. Makes them think twice."

Laurie was 10 years old when she was diagnosed with acute leukemia. "I wasn't worried," she said. "My mom said I wasn't going to die, and believe me, you do what my mom says or you're in deep trouble."

Dean was in and out of the hospital all the time. He had bone cancer, and had to have bone marrow samples taken month after month. He also had operations, radiation, chemotherapy—even amputations. He was stuck with needles all the time, X-rayed, abandoned by friends, spoiled, ignored, experimented on, and stared at. "I keep coming back here despite all the aggravation," he said. "I figure the doctors and the nurses couldn't make it without me. They take this whole thing too seriously. I decided it was my personal mission to make them lighten up."

It is true that these young people miss a lot of what we would call a "normal" life. But their attitude is not gloomy. They don't look back over what they missed, but instead they look forward toward what is to come. To them, life is to be lived regardless of the bumps, the detours, and the storms.

When these young people were told that they had a serious illness, many of them had the same reactions as people who are dying. They went through denial, saying, "This isn't happening to me." They went through the anger phase, too, where they tried to lay the blame on something. Bargaining and depression also hit all of them at some time. But none of them wasted much time on any of these phases. They arrived at acceptance very quickly, and then got on with the process of dealing with the changes in their lives. Their families, however, didn't always do as well.

One eight-year-old boy said, "I have leukemia because my mother lived near a nuclear power plant when she was pregnant with me. That's what my Grandma says."

Often the families of sick children blame themselves, the environment, bad laws, where they live, the doctors—you name it—for what has happened. This is often the reason why many young people prefer to deal with their illnesses by keeping a lot of their feelings to themselves. They've seen how upsetting it is to their parents.

"It was really hard on my mom," says Howie, a 12-year-old with kidney failure. "We were always waiting for a kidney that would match, and I cracked a lot of accident jokes that made her cry. I finally stopped because everyone around me was freaking out. But sometimes I just couldn't be so serious. I would think the joke to myself."

Howie was finally able to talk to a therapist

Some of us can live a long time, like Frances Swetland of Pennsylvania. She celebrated her 104th birthday in 1989.

at the hospital where he was on kidney dialysis.

"She said I was working out my fears," said Howie. "But at least she laughed with me."

When someone else in your family faces a serious illness, it is also a hard thing to deal with. It wrecks the original fabric of the family's life. Usually, with one person needing extensive care, the others get less attention. Again, as with everything else in life, this massive shift in lifestyle is easier to deal with if there is someone to talk to about feelings and fears.

Laurie's little brother was diagnosed as having leukemia when he was eight and she was twelve. Suddenly everything in Laurie's world turned upside down.

"My mother had just gone back to work, and we were planning this really neat vacation to Hawaii in the summer," said Laurie. "Then my brother John got sick. She had to quit her job. She's never home. Dad has to cook dinner half the time, and I usually end up cooking it the other half of the time. Sometimes she's gone for weeks at a time when they go to stay at the Ronald McDonald House in New York City."

Laurie felt neglected. Her mother was tired and worried and bad tempered a lot of the time. Her father had many more financial worries than he'd ever had before. Suddenly Laurie was forced to grow up and take on lots of responsibility that she didn't want.

"I really felt that the whole thing was John's fault," said Laurie. "And it sort of is. I mean it's because of him that we have no money, and I basically don't have a mother any more—not that it was John's fault that he got leukemia, but still...."

Laurie has a hard time talking about how she feels because there is a lot of guilt involved. After all, she is healthy, and he is sick. She feels badly that he's in so much pain, but she's tired of being neglected, too. Laurie also gets angry at John because he gets all the attention.

"Not only that," she said, "Everybody feels really sorry for him because he feels so sick, and he hurts a lot of the time. They get him all these great presents, and they forget about me. It's like they're saying, 'You have your health. You don't need anything else.' Well, sometimes I need things, too."

Laurie needed someone to talk to about her own feelings. She couldn't handle them by herself. Her grades began to fall. Even though she blamed this on the extra chores she had to do at home, the real cause lay in her increasing distraction and depression. Her teacher noticed and got the school counselor to talk with Laurie. She now goes to a support group for families of very sick people, and she's able to share a lot of her problems with young people who understand.

Sometimes adults in these young people's families can't help. They find it very hard to be supportive with their healthy children because they can barely manage to hold themselves together. That's why support groups can be so beneficial. There are many reasons why parents find it difficult to talk about the situation, but the most important ones are that they are either too frightened, too busy, or have a hard time communicating about anything at all. Young people often find it hard to keep trying anyway. But sometimes, after the initial shock wears off a bit, parents can start to talk to other members of the family about what's happening to them. It is always a good idea to keep the lines of family communication open—even if nothing too helpful happens at first.

In the meantime, however, it's important to find someone else to talk to like one of the doctors, a relative, a friend from school, or your clergyman. School counselors are also available for discussing problems. They are more than happy to help students get through a crisis.

One of the biggest reasons to find someone to talk to is that when a member of your family is extremely ill, it is a stressful time for everybody. Sometimes the adults in the house can start drinking excessively or become abusive. You will probably have very mixed feelings toward the sick per-

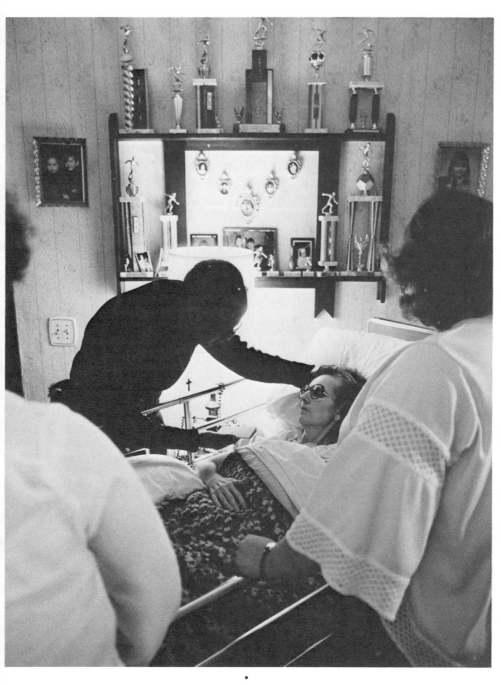

Dying at home, surrounded by loved ones, is becoming more acceptable in the 1980s and '90s, instead of waiting in an unfamiliar hospital where family and friends may only visit. Before the era of modern medicine, dying at home was normal, not an exception.

son like jealousy or wishing the person would die so that things will be normal again. Talking about these feelings can help you get your thoughts back in order and understand the new direction your family's lives are taking.

Benjamin

Benjamin's older brother Chris was in a car accident when Benjamin was 14 years old. He was paralyzed from the chest down. Not only did Chris's life change, but so did Benjamin's. Their mother now spends most of her time caring for her oldest boy, and everyone at home is usually badtempered. Benjamin is very angry at Chris.

"I know my Mom needs help, but sometimes I just can't stand going into Chris's room. It smells bad a lot," says Benjamin. "He's always so cheerful when I come to see him. But that always makes it worse."

Chris has basically come to accept the fact that he's paralyzed. He knows that with a lot of physical therapy he'll be able to use a wheelchair someday. This has given him tremendous hope. But for his family, things are always going to remain pretty much the same. Chris will always need a lot of care.

"I know this sounds awful, but what kind of a life is Chris going to ever have? Sometimes I wish he'd just died in the car crash," Benjamin says. "Whenever I think that, I want to run away from home. I feel like I can't face Chris. I think he'll be able to see what I'm thinking, and that's horrible."

Benjamin needs to talk to a counselor of some kind. He is very jealous of Chris's special needs, and also feels terrible guilt for wishing that Chris had died in the accident. If a therapist could get Chris and Benjamin to talk about what they're feeling, it might help Benjamin deal with how important life is to Chris. That way, Benjamin would also understand how important life is to everyone—regardless of the difficulties they face.

What Benjamin doesn't yet know, but what Chris has already found out, is that life is the most

All of us need love and comfort, no matter what our age. This woman has the friendship of a puppy in her nursing home. Caring for others, including pets, can be a very healthy prescription.

precious thing there is. Thinking, feeling, learning, understanding and giving and receiving love can give even the most curtailed life meaning and optimism. Perhaps if Benjamin allows himself to communicate with his older brother, he will learn what Chris has to teach him. And if he does, his life will be a much fuller and happier one.

VI. The Right To Live, The Right To Die

Many court battles have recently been fought over keeping people who are either extremely ill or in comas alive by means of modern technology. Sometimes terminally ill people want to have the right to end their own lives with dignity, and so do their families. Many people object to the artificial methods used to keep someone from dying a natural death. But this debate puts doctors and hospital staffs who are dedicated to preserving life in a difficult position. Unhooking dying people from machines that keep them alive could be considered murder under the law.

When life becomes a question of heartbeat and respiration, when there is no thinking, no joy, and no awareness (except perhaps of pain), is it still considered life? Is a person who is breathing only with the help of machines and not producing any brain waves truly alive? Some people do come out of comas, but many do not. Who has the right to decide if a person in a coma is worth keeping alive by mechanical means? Who can know whether a comatose person will ever wake up? Does a dying patient with no hope of being cured have the right to decide to end his or her own life? These are some questions being decided in courtrooms across the country.

The saddest part of these court battles is that the people involved feel that their own lives and the lives of their families are out of their hands. People reading about them feel the same way. They know that once they set foot in a hospital, most decisions regarding their fate are often taken away. Sometimes these decisions become the center of lawsuits, when doctors, patients and families disagree over the proper way to handle a grave illness. Everyone has an opinion, but no one really has the answers.

Just because someone is sick or dying doesn't mean they should have to give up their rights. And one of the most important freedoms we have is the right to choose the manner in which we handle our lives. As long as there is no harm done

A cemetery, like this one on Long Island, New York, is often called a "final resting place." Humans have buried the remains of their dead since prehistoric times.

to others or society, people should have that basic right until they die. The seriously ill or dying person knows how important each moment is, and how precious life is.

Some people believe that letting someone choose to disconnect life-support equipment is immoral. Some claim that *euthanasia* (the practice of painlessly putting someone to death to relieve an incurable illness) is criminal, or suicidal. Others feel that people have a right to say "when"—that they have lived long enough, and that some terminal forms of illness rob a person of their enjoyment of life. This will be a closely-watched issue in the 1990s.

One very interesting court case that received tremendous national attention focused on Ryan White, a hemophiliac. Ryan got AIDS from a blood transfusion when he was 14 years old. His school in Kokomo, Indiana, did not want an AIDS carrier in the classroom. His fellow students taunted him, and finally school officials barred him from attending classes. His family moved to Cicero, Illinois, where Ryan was accepted and allowed to go to school.

Because of the publicity surrounding the fight between the Whites and the Kokomo school board (which the Whites eventually won), Ryan was thrust into the national spotlight. He became a spokesperson for AIDS victims, along with famous sports figures, politicians, and rock stars. But the thing Ryan White wanted more than anything else was to be like other kids, go to school and live as normal a life as possible. As his best friend said, "He didn't want people to feel sorry for him. He hated that. He just wanted to be a regular kid."

In April 1990, Ryan White died. First Lady Barbara Bush, singers Michael Jackson and Elton John and many other famous people attended his funeral. Tributes poured in from all over the country, including the following. They are a tribute to a young man who learned to accept his own death, and taught many more about death as a part of life.

"Ryan has helped us understand the truth about AIDS, and he has shown all of us the strength and bravery of the human heart."

—President George Bush

"For reasons which we may never fully understand, Ryan's life was set on a course that no one could predict and which we could do precious little to affect....We owe it to Ryan to make sure that the fear and ignorance that chased him from his home and school will be eliminated. We owe it to Ryan to open our hearts and minds to those with AIDS. We owe it to Ryan to be

This crowd of more than 1,000 walked along a Los Angeles boulevard during a candlelit march honoring those who have died from AIDS. The spread of this disease has intensified awareness of "death with dignity" and the courage of those faced with terminal illness.

compassionate, caring and tolerant toward those with AIDS, their families and their friends."

—Former President Ronald Reagan

"Here's a kid who was 14 years old who led the nation by his example."

—Dr. Woodrow Myers, New York City health commissioner, former Indiana state health commissioner.

Life Is To Be Lived

Understanding one's own mortality makes it possible to deal with death—whether it be our own or someone close to us, whether it is expected or comes in a way that is sudden and shocking. As we can see by Ryan White's example, people can learn to deal with some very confusing aspects of life and death with a strong hand, and they can learn to enjoy life as it should be enjoyed: as fully as possible.

Glossary

AFTERLIFE. The religious belief that the soul or spirit goes to heaven or a place of peace to be reunited with others who have died.

AIDS (Acquired Immune Deficiency Syndrome). A disease that causes a breakdown of the body's immune system.

CHEMOTHERAPY. The use of chemical agents in the treatment or control of disease, especially cancer.

CREMATION. When the body of a dead person is burned to ashes rather than buried in a cemetary. Those who leave instructions to be cremated often have their ashes scattered over a special place from an airplane.

EUTHANASIA. To put to death painlessly; some terminally ill people wish to die instead of prolong their pain and suffering with medical machinery and drugs. Euthanasia (sometimes called "mercy killing") is at the center of a legal and moral controversy in the United States today.

FUNERAL. A service for the family and friends of one who has died; the rituals at a funeral may or may not have a religious tone. The purpose is for the survivors to comfort each other after the loss of a loved one.

HOSPICE. A homelike facility that cares for the terminally ill.

LEUKEMIA. A disease in the body's tissues that manufacture blood cells.

REINCARNATION. The religious belief that every one has a soul that survives the death of the body, and that all souls are reborn into a new body to live another physical life. Followers of the Hindu religion especially believe in reincarnation.

TERMINAL ILLNESS. An illness from which a person is unlikely to recover.

Bibliography

Baron, Connie. *The Physically Disabled.* Crestwood House, 1988

Bombeck, Erma. *I Want to Grow Hair, I Want to Grow Up, I Want to Go to Boise.* Children Surviving Cancer, Harper & Row, 1989

Burns, Sheila L. *Cancer, Understanding And Fighting It.* Julian Messner, N.Y. 1982

Kubler-Ross, Elisabeth. *On Children and Death.* Macmillan, 1983

Kubler-Ross, Elisabeth. *On Death And Dying.* Macmillan, 1969

LeShan, Eda J. "When A Parent Is Very Sick." *Atlantic Monthly* 1986

Marsoli, Lisa Ann. *Things To Know About Death and Dying.* Silver Burdett Company, N.J. 1985

Richler, Elisabeth. *Losing Someone You Love, When A Sister or Brother Dies.* G.P. Putnams, N.Y. 1986

Rofers, Eric E. *The Kids Book About Death and Dying, By and For Kids.* Little Brown & Compnay, Boston 1985

Index

Picture Credits

AP/Wide World Photos	12, 39, 45, 50, 54, 56-57
Dan Chidester/The Image Works	27
Howard Dratch/The Image Works	25
Robert V. Eckert Jr./EKM-Nepenthe	29
Robert W. Ginn/EKM-Nepenthe	9
Tim Jewett/EKM-Nepenthe	17
Jack Spratt/The Image Works	48
Topham/The Image Works	35